How to Widen Participation

A Guide to Good Practice

'We know how to widen participation – now we need to make it happen'

Helena Kennedy QC

London: The Stationery Office

Contents

Preface

Throughout the work of the Widening Participation Committee, we were impressed by the many and varied ways in which colleges and other providers bring new learners into further education and help them to succeed. Through their ingenuity, imagination and skill, many colleges are reaching people who would otherwise not have considered making education part of their lives.

The case studies in this guide provide much to celebrate. They have been gathered in a systematic way by the Further Education Funding Council's inspectorate to illustrate different aspects of the characteristics of good practice the committee identified. The illustrations have been drawn from a sample of institutions for which the Council has formal responsibilities for quality assessment. These case studies are not, by any means, the only examples of good practice in the further education sector. We also know that there is wonderful work outside the sector. Much more could have been included if space had allowed and comparable evidence from elsewhere had been available. The evidence confirms our view that considerable expertise in ways of widening participation already exists, but much more needs to be done.

The fact is that good practice in widening participation is patchy. Strategies for widening participation are unevenly developed nationally, regionally and within individual colleges and other provision. Our report, *Learning Works*, published in July 1997, chiefly addressed the national and regional action necessary to widen participation. The aim of this guide is to provide a resource for those responsible for widening participation in colleges and other organisations. It suggests what a provider needs to do in order to widen participation with the needs of the learner always at the forefront.

I am pleased to present this guide to you and hope that you will find it a valuable tool in your work in years to come.

Helena Kennedy

Helena Kennedy QC

Foreword

Colleges intent on widening participation may identify with President Roosevelt's assertion that:

> ***'The test of our progress is not whether we add more to the abundance of those who have much; it is whether we provide enough for those who have too little'.***

The content of this guide is proof that some colleges are making a significant contribution to redressing educational inequality and injustice. The analysis of inspection evidence confirms one of the Widening Participation Committee's main conclusions that 'we know how to widen participation now we need to make it happen'. The guide to good practice should help colleges to evaluate strategies developed by many different providers and adapt and apply them to their own provision.

What is needed

Across the further education sector:

- more systematic strategies are needed to address persistent patterns of under-participation and under-achievement among some groups
- some innovative and different approaches are needed to tackle under-participation and under-achievement
- the proposed common standards in widening participation need to be achieved in all colleges
- colleges need to set themselves further and more challenging standards and targets
- more rigorous methods are needed to measure and report progress in widening participation at college, local, regional and national levels.

The Council is supporting action to widen participation in several ways during 1997-98. These are:

- the funding of a number of pilot local strategic partnerships which will draw up and implement plans for widening participation in their locality
- the introduction of a new learning pathway to meet the needs of under-represented learners aged 18 and over
- a national inspectorate exercise to focus on successful methods of teaching and ways of improving learners' achievement.

The strategic partnership plans will help to improve access, achievement and progression for groups who are underrepresented and/or who underachieve in further education. The new learning pathway will include accredited guidance, tutorial and learning support and will help to increase retention and achievement rates for learners from underrepresented groups.

The Council's inspectorate will continue to monitor the effectiveness of practice in widening participation as an integral part of its inspection of colleges, as well as carrying out a national survey of developments in widening participation.

The Widening Participation Committee's report, *Learning Works*, affirms the central role that further education has in widening participation for the nation. The sector is well placed to build on its existing successes to provide routes for all to increased personal fulfilment, educational achievement and social and economic prosperity.

David Melville

Introduction

This guide is designed to share good practice identified in *Learning Works*, published in June 1997, the main report of the Widening Participation Committee chaired by Helena Kennedy QC. That publication made the case for widening access to further education, to meet national needs as well as individual needs, and to promote social and economic progress and prosperity.

The guide aims to be of practical help in bringing a wider spectrum of the population into further education, and in helping them to achieve and to progress to employment or further study. By developing their capacity and enthusiasm for learning, successful participation will ensure they are motivated to seek out further learning opportunities, both for themselves and for their families, thus helping to create a self-perpetuating learning society. The guide offers some answers to the most commonly-asked questions about widening participation.

Whilst the guide is aimed primarily at colleges within the further education sector, the principles it suggests would also be useful to other providers of post-16 education, such as companies, training and enterprise councils (TECs), local education authorities (LEAs) and voluntary organisations. The guide sets out to help colleges to:

- review their own progress and achievements in widening participation
- learn from good practice developed by other providers of post-16 education
- plan future strategies for widening participation
- develop systems for assuring quality, and conduct self-assessments
- raise the profile and status of activities which widen participation.

Widening participation is an essential, but not an easy task. Efforts to widen participation can be both painstaking and unrewarding, but can also result in success stories of the most inspiring kind. The guide will help colleges to respond to the challenges they face in widening participation.

Throughout the guide, the term 'colleges' is used in a generic sense, to refer to all providers of further education, including external institutions and independent specialist colleges. Similarly the word 'learner' applies to all those who are participating in a learning activity.

What does widening participation mean?

Widening participation means 'access, achievement and progression'. It means bringing more students from underrepresented and disadvantaged groups into education and training; ensuring that these students stay on their programmes; extending the ways through which they can learn and achieve; and ensuring that they progress to suitable destinations.

Why widen participation?

Over half our young people leave school in need of compensatory education. They enter adult life inadequately equipped with the skills needed to participate effectively in the economy and society. Most adults receive no further learning opportunities after completing their initial education and training. The further education sector is a mass provider of education, offering opportunities for many to succeed. It now needs to open its doors to a wider range of people if more are to contribute effectively to the economic and social health of the nation and realise their potential.

Further education is in a prime position to explode the belief that 'if at first you don't succeed . . . you don't succeed'. In many colleges, more and more people are succeeding in education. These colleges have created a potent blend of opportunities, encouragement and support which has worked for many who believed that 'education is for other people'. But a more consistent and coherent approach is needed to create a nation of lifelong learners if we are to achieve economic prosperity and maintain social cohesion.

Most colleges are committed to widening participation. Many long-established colleges have continued to reflect in their aims the democratic origins of further education in the working men's colleges and mechanics' institutes of the nineteenth century. Other more recently established colleges have followed suit with mission statements and policies that aim to widen participation, promote equal opportunities and serve the local community – goals which are now included in the Council's criteria for self-assessment.

In *Learning Works*, the Widening Participation Committee made the case that:

- further education must be at the heart of any project for the national regeneration
- learning for work and learning for life are inseparable
- learning is a weapon against poverty and the route to participation and active citizenship.

Learning Works outlines examples where colleges recruit as learners people who do not usually participate in further education, and enable them to achieve and progress to more advanced education, employment or other fulfilling goals. It is this good practice that the Widening Participation Committee urges the sector to build upon and expand.

Who is underrepresented in further education?

In recent years, colleges have recruited increasing numbers to courses. However, they have been less successful in enabling learners from groups that have not usually been present in further education to enrol and achieve. Some groups remain underrepresented in further education. Few members of such groups participate, or only do so within a narrow range of learning, or underachieve. These groups include:

- people without qualifications
- unemployed people
- some groups of women, such as those in low-income groups, and those who are lone parents
- some groups of men, including white men in low-income groups
- some minority ethnic groups, including refugees
- those over 50 years old
- people with literacy and/or numeracy difficulties
- people with learning difficulties and/or disabilities from minority ethnic groups
- people with profound and multiple learning difficulties and/or disabilities
- adults with mental illness
- young people with emotional and behavioural difficulties
- ex-offenders
- part-time and temporary workers
- unskilled manual workers.

The Widening Participation Committee identified low previous educational achievement and low income as the key factors in non-participation.

Some groups of people tend to underachieve in further education even when they do enrol. In 1994-95, an average of 65 per cent of college students who completed courses achieved their qualification aim. Certain groups of students are more likely not to finish their courses and some, even if they complete their course, tend to achieve less well than others. Nationally, college data show that compared with other students:

- adults on full-time or part-time courses who receive some kind of benefit have significantly higher withdrawal rates and lower achievement rates
- adults on courses in literacy, numeracy and English for speakers of other languages have higher withdrawal rates
- withdrawal rates are higher for students from some minority ethnic groups such as male black Caribbean students, other black students and full-time students of Pakistani origin
- achievement rates are lower for some minority ethnic groups such as black African and black Caribbean students, and also for Indian students studying part time
- achievement rates are lower for male full-time students than female full-time students.

In order to achieve wider participation, colleges need to analyse their own data to identify any common patterns in recruitment, withdrawal and achievement. National data give the starting-point for such an analysis.

What are the challenges of widening participation?

Evidence presented to the Widening Participation Committee from over 400 inspections and 40 special visits to colleges shows that generally, the steps colleges take to widen participation are not as comprehensive or as wide-ranging as they could be. More colleges must establish strategies for widening participation which are comprehensive, rigorous and systematic. The challenge is for more colleges to:

- identify the needs of those who do not usually participate in further education in their local area
- create appropriate programmes of study to meet these needs
- provide the right kinds of guidance and support
- ensure that such learners are successful in gaining qualifications and achieving their goals and ambitions
- enable such learners to progress to more advanced education, training or employment.

In some colleges there are significant disparities between the college's mission statement and its ultimate success in widening participation. This can be because colleges preserve systems and procedures which in practice restrict participation. The gap between theory and practice may arise because:

- well-intentioned college mission statements may not be supported by the necessary strategic planning and systems to put them into practice
- efforts to widen participation may not be consistent across the college
- the college may not actively seek out non-participants in its locality and provide suitable opportunities for them
- the college's responsiveness may be restricted to providing for the more vocal local communities and employers
- provision for underrepresented groups may not be consistent over time
- there may be over-dependence on short-term project funding for initiatives to widen participation
- the aim of widening participation may be new to the college.

Strategies for widening participation are developed unevenly across England. In many areas of the country initiatives are thinly spread. The greatest concentrations of activity in widening participation are in the north of England, the Midlands, and London.

What is good practice in widening participation?

General further education, tertiary, agricultural and adult residential colleges have created strategies to widen participation and some have developed innovative and highly successful practices. Initiatives to widen participation which consistently work include:

- access to higher education courses which enable learners with few or no qualifications to succeed in their studies and progress
- community outreach provision which recruits people who initially would not consider going to college, and helps them to gain qualifications and to progress to work or more advanced courses
- provision which includes guidance and support as an integral part of courses, and which promotes learners' achievements and progression to more advanced study or employment.

Colleges which have achieved most in widening participation have:

- underpinned their commitment to widen participation with related policies, strategic objectives, operational plans, funding strategies and quality assurance arrangements
- developed an explicit focus on improving the achievements of people who do not usually participate in further education, not just on 'bringing them in'
- set up strategies for widening participation which are central to the college's activities and not reliant on marginalised special initiatives
- learned from effective practice in one part of the college and spread initiatives to other areas
- disseminated effective practice developed in other colleges
- set standards and targets for widening participation and reviewed progress against these
- secured the support and commitment of governors, teachers and other staff for widening participation.

The Widening Participation Committee's extensive work identified some of the characteristics of good practice which provide an effective framework for helping colleges to widen participation.

Characteristics of good practice in widening participation

1. marketing is planned and based on intelligence
2. there are strategies for contacting non-participants
3. good quality information and guidance is readily available and impartial
4. there is effective support for learning
5. financial and practical support is provided
6. there is an appropriate and relevant curriculum which enables learners to progress
7. there is effective teaching and learning
8. there are mechanisms for recording learners' achievements which acknowledge all learning, are meaningful to learners and are recognised by employers, education providers and others
9. management information is accurate and used to evaluate learners' progress and other aspects of provision.

How To Widen Participation

How can participation be widened?

Colleges can widen participation by ensuring that:

- strategies for widening participation are threaded through all areas of the college's work
- barriers to participation and achievement are successfully identified and removed
- the characteristics of good practice are used to evaluate and improve provision.

The characteristics of good practice are interrelated and add up to more than the sum of their parts. The different elements of good practice need to be seen as aspects of a whole process. They should both underpin and drive organisational culture, strategy, structure and practice.

Widening participation using the characteristics of good practice

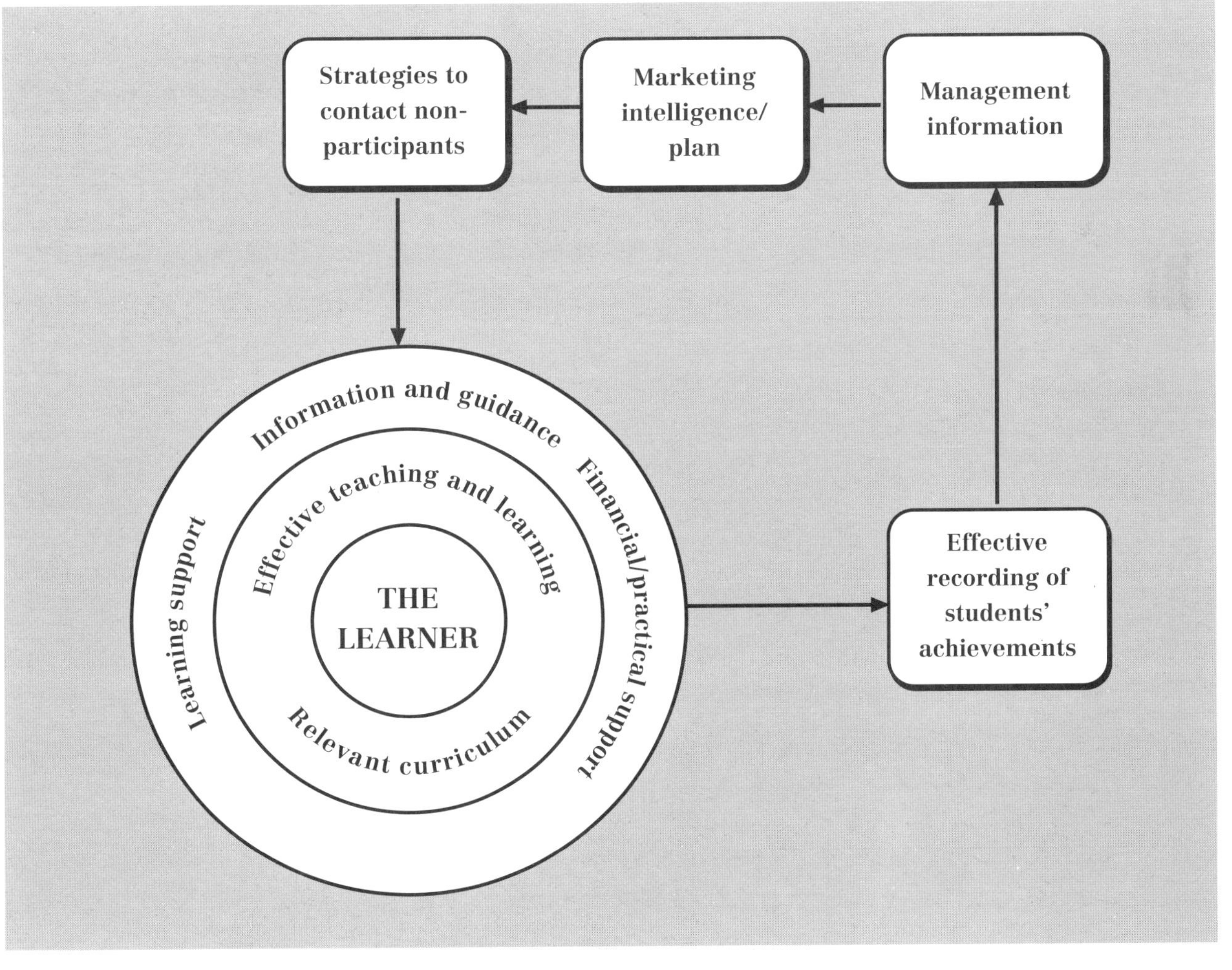

Strategies for widening participation will be most effective when developed within local or regional partnerships with, for instance, LEAs, TECs, voluntary organisations, employers, other colleges, schools and trade unions. This will mean developing joint policies and plans with other providers, and the sharing of good practice and resources.

Colleges will seek to:

- set clear and achievable strategic objectives which relate to good practice
- take practical steps to meet the needs of groups who do not usually enter further education, for example, through the choice of teaching and learning strategies
- support learners effectively and enable them to achieve
- review systematically their progress in widening participation and set new and more challenging targets and standards for future developments
- establish the new learning pathway for adult learners from underrepresented groups, where guidance and support are integral parts of accredited programmes.

The Widening Participation Committee has made specific recommendations to the Council to support the new learning pathway. The Council hopes to implement this recommendation from January 1998.

The new learning pathway:

1. is for learners aged 18 and over with low prior attainment
2. comprises provision which meets quality criteria based on good practice characteristics
3. offers opportunities at foundation, intermediate and advanced level
4. provides individual learning programmes
5. delivers a planned programme of accredited learning support
6. leads to recognised qualifications.

How can success in widening participation be assessed and measured?

Colleges intent on widening participation can:

- assess current achievements and weaknesses in widening participation using the standards set against the characteristics in the section on Good Practice in Action (see page 13)
- set more challenging standards and targets to help make further improvements
- measure progress through the analysis of statistical data.

To widen participation colleges, the Council and the government need also to set higher standards and demonstrate the progress made. They all need to be able to answer the critical question:

> *'Are the energies, efforts and resources given to widening participation yielding positive outcomes for the learners from underrepresented groups?'*

Assessing progress using standards

The Widening Participation Committee has endorsed a set of standards relating to the characteristics of good practice in widening participation. These standards are set out in the tables in the section on Good Practice in Action.

The tables present:

- the needs of the learner
- the role of the provider
- standards for colleges
- sources of evidence.

The standards will help colleges and the Council to assess and demonstrate how successfully participation is being widened in further education. They will also help colleges to develop further quality assurance and self-assessment processes which have a clear focus on widening participation.

The proposed standards focus on outcomes rather than processes. They provide benchmarks for each of the characteristics of good practice and make explicit the level of performance required. Colleges can ensure that they are meeting these minimum standards and, in addition, set their own more specific and challenging standards to help make further improvements in widening participation.

Measuring progress using statistical data

The Widening Participation Committee has recommended that local strategic partnerships should set targets for widening participation among underrepresented groups in their areas. Targets which would help individual colleges and groups of providers measure their progress and performance in widening participation could include:

- the percentage increase in the number of learners enrolled from nationally and locally determined underrepresented groups
- the percentage increase in the number of learners in the identified groups who achieve their qualification aim
- the percentage increase in the number of learners in the identified groups who progress to employment, further or higher education.

The Widening Participation Committee has developed a framework which enables colleges and other providers to set targets and measure their performance in widening participation. The framework provides a means of setting baseline figures against which progress can be measured.

The framework draws on existing data provided to the Council by colleges through the individualised student record (ISR).

It is designed to:

- measure the key elements of widening participation at national level
- enable colleges and other providers at local level to measure how far they have widened participation.

The framework is supported by tables in appendix 4 showing the national participation rates in further education analysed by age, sex and ethnicity, and also according to other factors such as receipt of benefits and postcode. The tables cover recruitment, retention and progression, and each is accompanied by a brief commentary explaining how they could be used by colleges. These tables will be updated annually. A separate volume, *Widening Participation in Further Education: Statistical Evidence*, provides greater detail on the methodology underlying the statistics.

It is important that colleges set their targets according to local conditions, rather than striving only to match national benchmarks. The national data can be used in setting the context for their activities.

Framework

The Framework for Measuring Participation

Stage of student progress	Monitoring characteristics	National baseline table
Recruitment	age, sex, ethnicity	tables 1 to 3
	level and type of qualifications by age, sex, ethnicity	table 4; local data by sex, ethnicity
	prior attainment by age group or if not available	table 5 for 16 and 17 year olds
	- adults students receiving benefit*	tables 6 to 9
	- postcodes (level of deprivation)*	table 10
Retention	age, sex, ethnicity	tables 11 to 12
	level and type of qualifications by age, sex, ethnicity	table 13; local data by sex, ethnicity
	prior attainment	insufficient national data available 1995-96
	students receiving benefit*	table 14
	postcodes (level of deprivation)*	to be monitored locally
Achievement	age, sex, ethnicity	tables 15 to 16
	level and type of qualifications by age, sex, ethnicity	table 17; local data by sex, ethnicity
	prior attainment	insufficient national data available 1995-96
	students receiving benefit*	table 18
	postcodes (level of deprivation)*	to be monitored locally
Progression and destinations	level and type of qualifications, age, sex and ethnicity	table 19; can also be monitored in more detail locally

* see separate volumes: *Widening Participation in Further Education: Statistical Evidence* and *Identifying and Addressing Needs: A Practical Guide* (FEFC 1997)

A cycle of activities

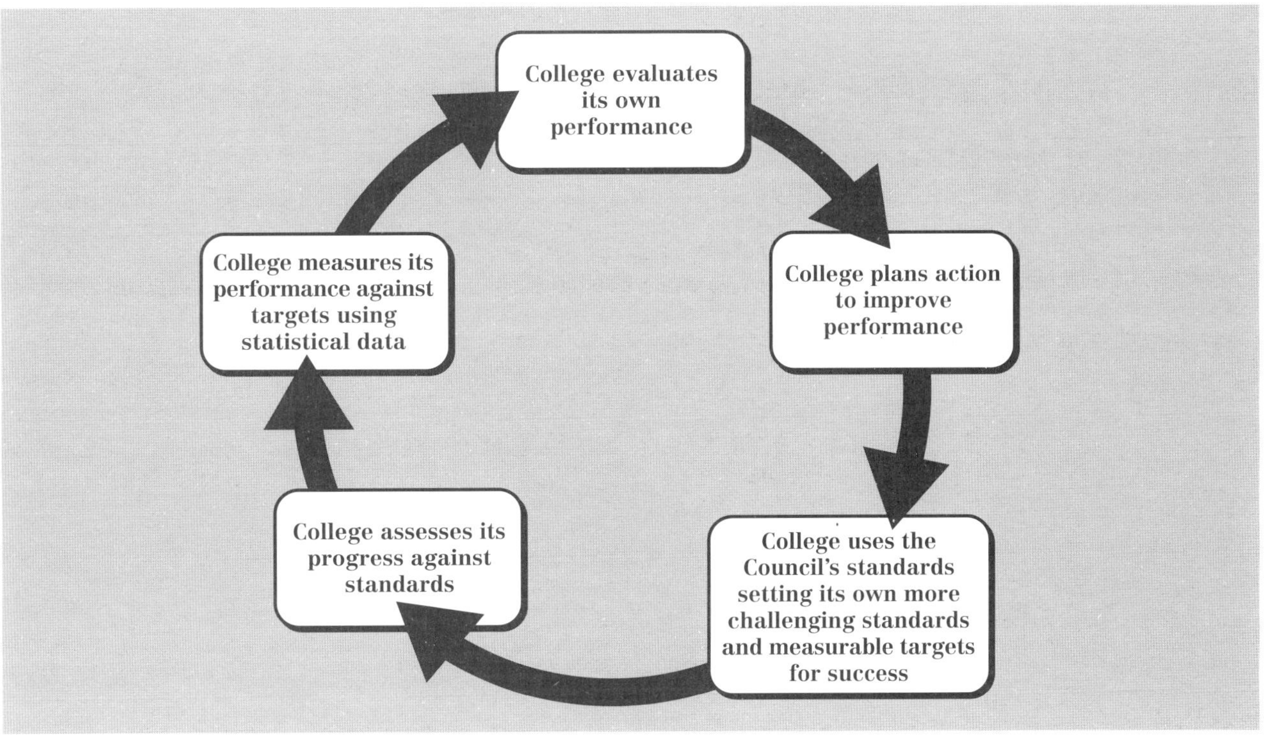

A cycle of activities to widen participation

Colleges will need to:

- build arrangements for widening participation into their regular planning, reporting and quality assurance systems
- use the national standards and establish their own standards, assess and measure their own performance and make improvements in widening participation
- identify a person with overall responsibility for widening participation across the college who is charged with ensuring that performance in widening participation is assessed and measured, that achievements are evaluated and that changes and further improvements are made
- present regular evaluative reports to governors on progress made in widening participation.

In the most effective practice colleges will have a planned cycle of activities for widening participation.

Colleges can map their progress in widening participation by measuring achievements in domains relevant to each of the characteristics of good practice. Representing progress on a 'widening participation grid' will help to illustrate aspects of widening participation that are on target, and those which are not. At present, most colleges are more successful in achieving progress in the areas covered by the first few characteristics of good practice. Their efforts and achievements tail off towards characteristic nine.

Charting progress in widening participation

The following chart gives examples of the targets set by a college for widening participation. The college has identified two groups of people who are underrepresented, residents of a particular housing estate, and young black men aged 18 to 24. They have set targets against each of the characteristics to focus activities for these groups. In addition, they have set some general targets for teaching and learning, and recording achievements. As each target is achieved, it can be crossed through or ticked to show progress. More detailed action plans are in place for each target with criteria for success and a system for monitoring the action taken.

Charting Progress

✓ Targets Achieved

Characteristic	Marketing plan and intelligence	Contacting non-participants	Information and guidance	Learning support
Target 1	■ enrolments from Greenbanks estate increased by 50%	■ outreach programmes set up in one homeless project and two primary schools in Greenbanks district ✓	■ advice and guidance sessions provided in Greenbanks outreach centres monthly	■ literacy and numeracy support built into Greenbanks outreach courses ✓
Target 2	■ enrolments by black male students aged 18-24 for level 2 skills courses increased by 30% ✓	■ introductory sessions set up at two local factories and two youth and community centres ✓	■ advice and guidance sessions form part of work-based and community-based introductory sessions ✓	■ literacy and numeracy support built into college-based stage of programme ✓
Target 3				
Target 4				
Target 5				
Target 6				
Target 7 and so on...				

Financial and practical support	Relevant curriculum	Effective teaching and learning	Effective recording of achievement	Accurate management information
staff planned ways of meeting support needs with each student on Greenbanks outreach courses ✓	curriculum options for college-based taster courses based on negotiation with Greenbanks students ✓	staff development for four Greenbanks outreach teachers on basic skills teaching ✓	develop Open College Network accredited modules on personal and career development for all outreach courses ✓	80% successful completion rate for Greenbanks students ✓
welfare officer to attend introductory sessions at each community venue to offer financial advice ✓	new learning pathway set up with skills-based options within hours suitable for those on benefits ✓	schemes of work designed to accommodate different levels of prior experience ✓	NVQ units and whole qualifications are offered ✓	% successful completion rate of target group matches that of other level 2 students
		staff development for all staff teaching foundation level students ✓	develop college-designed record of achievement for all level 2 courses	
		opportunity for course teams to identify and share good practice in differentiated learning		

Good Practice in Action

The characteristics of good practice, key recommendations, case studies and views of students ('students' voices')

The charts which follow provide an analysis of each characteristic of good practice in widening participation. The needs of the learner and the role of the provider are identified. A set of standards is provided, with evidence to show that the standards have been achieved. Examples of good practice from inspection evidence and the views of students illustrate each characteristic. These examples are typical of good practice found in many other colleges not specifically named. While some are innovative, many are tried and tested practice.

Good Practice in Action

Characteristic one

Marketing is planned and based on intelligence

Needs of learner	Role of provider	Standards for colleges	Evidence
opportunities to express views about what kinds of education they are interested in or need	identify under-represented groups	groups of prospective learners under-represented locally and nationally are identified	a marketing plan which includes a clear focus on underrepresented groups
to be sought by providers as many are unlikely to make the first move	identify the learning needs of these groups	educational needs and interests of learners from underrepresented groups are analysed	the marketing strategy for these groups is based on market research and intelligence
	develop strategies to reach these groups	targets are set for recruiting these learners in all parts of the college	reports of visits to local communities to find out the learning needs and interests of learners underrepresented groups
		performance in recruiting these learners is measured and evaluated	evaluative reports on the effectiveness of the marketing strategy
		success rates among these learners are measured and evaluated	quantifiable data of the outcomes of strategies in terms of both enrolment and success

Key Recommendations:

- colleges need to put more energy into identifying groups who are underrepresented and identifying their learning needs and interests
- colleges should use information about the labour market, the local population, and their learner population for marketing purposes
- colleges need to develop strategic partnerships with other agencies to identify under-represented groups and their needs

Case Studies

Examples of Good Practice

A community needs analysis

Nelson and Colne College's annual community needs analysis matches its learner profile with that of the local community. Census data, employment and unemployment data are used to build up the picture. By mapping the ethnicity, sex, age, attendance by postcode, mode of attendance and the previous school of existing learners, the college identifies groups that are underrepresented. Strategies can then be devised to attract underrepresented groups into further education.

An attitude survey

At East Durham Community College a team of eight community development officers liaise with community groups, establish needs and develop a relevant curriculum. This liaison includes a formal committee of elected town and parish councillors who advise the college on the kind of curriculum which is appropriate to their own area. Each individual community has their own prospectus, and enrolment and delivery takes place in a range of outreach centres including village halls, community centres and youth clubs.

Setting targets for recruitment

Northern College for Residential Adult Education Ltd has a comprehensive range of performance criteria by which to judge its success in relation to widening participation: these include targets for recruitment by age, sex, social class, ethnicity, disability and previous qualifications. The college targets men and women over 20 who are disadvantaged and who would benefit from a period of intensive residential study. It uses such data for measuring its success.

Community development

Greenwich Community College runs a substantial housing estates community development programme for over 2,000 residents as part of the local authority's strategy to combat poverty and encourage economic regeneration. The programme helps residents to identify their own needs and build up their skills. Community development work effectively uncovers adults' interests by engaging them in informal learning such as participating in tenants' groups as well as in more formal learning opportunities such as courses in creative writing, computing and basic skills.

Students' Voices:

- *'The fact that the college held a meeting with us in the community showed they do care and they will listen to what we want. Most officials wouldn't bother because were not white and polite like their neighbourhoods.'*
- *'The college took the trouble to find out about travelling communities and to understand our way of life. A development worker came to our vans and talked to us about what we'd like to learn.'*

Good Practice in Action

Characteristic Two

There are strategies for contacting non-participants

Needs of learner	Role of provider	Standards for colleges	Evidence
opportunities to find out about college's provision without going in to college	work with local or regional partners to develop strategies for contacting underrepresented groups	effective strategies are in place for informing underrepresented groups about learning opportunities	promotional materials and activities for underrepresented groups
information which is provided in a user-friendly format	develop learning opportunities which minimise barriers to participation and appeal to the target group through such means as: outreach projects, activities with schools, non-schedule 2 courses, community-based activities	barriers to participation are identified	a list of barriers for specific groups with rectifying strategies
opportunities to identify and help overcome barriers they may face when returning to study		barriers to participation are addressed in the design of learning opportunities	records of collaboration between the college and other agencies to reach underrepresented groups
opportunities to enter study which are motivating, non-threatening, in the right place at the right time, and which offer a perceived benefit			evaluative reports demonstrating the effectiveness of strategies to reach non-participants

Key Recommendations:

- different kinds of publicity need developing; glossy productions can deter some learners, and there should be planned word-of-mouth campaigns using people from similar backgrounds to the target groups
- colleges should identify potential partners who have effective links with underrepresented groups
- colleges need to be open, reciprocal and involve other agencies in the planning and management of provision
- provision should be planned to overcome identified barriers and encourage participation.

Case Studies

Examples of Good Practice

Outreach in rural areas

Northumberland College has eight outreach centres which provide further education. Three community guidance workers provide impartial advice about careers and education and help to plan the courses offered in the centres. These workers liaise with community groups, assess the needs of the community and build networks in the locality. Centres have facilities for open and distance learning and video-conferencing.

Taking learning to the learner

'Learning World', a co-operative venture between Gateshead College and the University of Sunderland, is based in the Metro Centre in Gateshead. The shop-front location and flexible delivery of courses at weekends or in the evenings, as intensive study blocks or as more traditional part-time study, enable many people to enrol who would not join more conventionally organised provision. Some courses, for example, computing training for staff working in local voluntary organisations, are designed specifically to meet the needs of employers.

Partnerships with schools and local communities

Joseph Chamberlain Sixth Form College is a key member of the Balsall Heath Education Network which works with parents and carers of primary and secondary school pupils. A pilot project of courses in English for speakers of other languages and a course based on the RSA National Skills Profile for parents and carers in one school has resulted from the work of the network. The college also provides courses targeted at the Chinese and Yemeni communities in its area through the network.

Increasing participation amongst minority ethnic groups

The Oldham College's community education unit works closely with the training and enterprise council (TEC), Oldham Metropolitan Borough, local schools, Pakistani, Bengali and Indian community groups and employers. The unit has developed programmes in community languages and in English for local employers. It delivers programmes in community centres, schools, workplaces, church halls, women's centres and in a bus adapted to be a 'travelling classroom'.

Students' Voices:

- *'The community worker is just like us: he chatted to us about what we might like to do and really listened to our suggestions.'*
- *'I couldn't afford the bus fares to get to the college, but now they've set up a centre right here and I have given it a try. I've met new friends and it feels friendly and safe here.'*

Good Practice in Action

Characteristic Three

Good quality information and guidance is readily available and impartial

Needs of learner	Role of provider	Standards for colleges	Evidence
initial information and guidance at a convenient location	ensure information reaches all learners	there are strategies for providing information and guidance to learners from underrepresented groups	analyses of evaluations show information and guidance is readily available and useful
help in understanding what programmes and support are available and where programmes can lead	develop a guidance policy with underpinning principles which sets standards	these learners make informed choices about studies and career goals	learners' records of achievement and action plans
support in making informed choices at all stages; pre-entry, on course and on exit	train staff to deliver good quality guidance	they have access to guidance before enrolling, during their programmes and when preparing to leave college	guidance policy and standards
	record the needs of targeted learners	guidance staff review and develop the effectiveness of their practice with learners from under-represented groups	staff development records
	collaborate with others to distribute information and provide initial guidance		reports on the quality of guidance practices and summaries of the needs of targeted learners
	make an agreement with a careers service which includes monitoring systems		documents demonstrating collaboration with other organisations
	allow learners to evaluate the quality of their guidance		an appropriate agreement with a careers service

Key Recommendations:

- colleges should ensure good quality guidance is offered to learners from underrepresented groups at all stages
- guidance services must be available to all, including part-time and outreach learners
- guidance services need to be designed to match the needs of learners from different backgrounds
- the effectiveness of guidance services for underrepresented groups should be evaluated.

Case Studies

Examples of Good Practice

Initial guidance

The Cathedral Centre, Bradford, was established to provide a Christian response to unemployment and offer training and advice services. Every Wednesday morning, staff offer a tour of the centre and informal presentations about courses and support offered and facilities at the centre. Prospective learners meet learners on courses and see the teaching rooms and equipment and they are each offered individual guidance before they enrol on courses.

Advice and guidance in the community

The Southall Next Step Centre, run in conjunction with Ealing Tertiary College, offers one-to-one information, advice and guidance on a drop-in and appointments basis at three levels to suit adults' different needs. Level one is information only provided by reception staff, level two is a 15-minute initial guidance interview with an adviser, and level three is an hour's consultation with an adviser. Centre staff speak the main community languages such as Hindi, Punjabi, Gujarati, and Urdu and they can contact colleagues for help with other languages.

An integrated strategy for information, advice and guidance

Lewisham College has developed an integrated strategy for advice and guidance designed to tackle barriers to access and improve completion rates. A guidance map has been produced showing the different types of counselling and guidance available in the college and how they are provided. Guidance staff collaborate with the teaching faculties to co-ordinate support, and there are close links with external agencies.

On-course guidance in outreach provision

Guidance staff from Gloucestershire College of Arts and Technology visit outreach centres part way through a course to inform learners about college guidance services, provide relevant information and guidance materials and demonstrate computerised guidance packages such as 'Job File Explorer' on portable laptops provided by funding from the local education authority. Individual guidance appointments are offered to learners and can take place in the outreach location.

Students' Voices:

- *'I didn't have a clue about what I could do. But the college arranged for me to see one of their guidance workers who talked it all through with me very carefully and told me what was available – not only at this college but also at other ones in the area.'*
- *'I just popped into the college advice shop on impulse and picked up some leaflets: the person behind the desk was very knowledgeable and well, here I am!'*

Good Practice in Action

Characteristic Four

There is effective support for learning

Needs of learner	Role of provider	Standards for colleges	Evidence
help to identify own strengths and weaknesses and develop an action plan	ensure learning support needs of learners from underrepresented groups	the learning support needs of learners from under-represented groups are systematically assessed on all programmes	summaries of the support needs of learners from under-represented groups
opportunities to remedy weaknesses through additional tuition or practice	support effectively learners with learning difficulties and/or disabilities on mainstream and separate specialist programmes	strategies are in place to meet the learning support needs of those learners	policies and strategies for college-wide learning support evaluations of learning support and tutorial programme
access to personal support	create a tutorial system which meets the needs of all learners provide access to professional counselling	the effectiveness of learning support for learners from underrepresented groups is evaluated including the use of learners' views	learners' individual support plans learners' individual action plans tutorial policy and framework
individual meetings with tutor to review progress	monitor the effectiveness of learning support	all learners are satisfied with the quality of support they receive	summary records of counselling services

Key Recommendations:

- learning support needs should be identified in ways which are not threatening and which do not suggest that learners are inadequate; plans for support should include building on strengths
- learners should be actively involved in planning how they are supported and participate in reviewing arrangements
- colleges should not assume that certain types of learners need support; they may not
- support should be tailored to meet individual needs; plans should be made to equip learners with the skills to use support materials independently and to move beyond the need for additional learning support.

Case Studies

Examples of Good Practice

Encouraging learners to use support services

Birkenhead Sixth Form College shows new learners an analysis of the range of learners who used support services during the previous year. New learners get the message very quickly that learners on all levels of courses use support and that, at some time in their learning, they are likely to need extra help.

Identifying basic skills support needs

Learners enrolling on literacy and numeracy classes at Stoke-on-Trent College are invited to talk to teachers about printed materials such as public signs, train timetables, food labels, television listings from magazines and articles from newspapers. They are asked to read some parts of them. Learners appreciate talking about their reading and writing skills rather than being plunged straight into written tests. They like the friendly and informal approach of the teachers and the real-life reading materials. The assessment process makes learners feel less nervous and more enthusiastic about studying.

Learning support as part of the curriculum

At Thurrock College learning support is integral to courses. Screening strategies and materials are developed by each curriculum area to identify learners' basic skills needs in the context of their learning goals. A study skills learning plan is drawn up with the active involvement and agreement of the learner, with agreed targets and a record of work. Basic skills are developed in subject classes and, in addition, learners can use a study skills centre run by full-time centre staff and vocational staff appointed from different curriculum areas.

A black mentoring service for black learners

City College, Manchester, has a well-established mentoring service to support learners from minority ethnic groups. Mentors are staff or community volunteers who are knowledgeable and experienced in the learner's subject area and/or their intended career area. Mentors work with learners and teachers to identify any barriers to study and achievement. Potential problems are diagnosed and academic, welfare, careers and personal counselling support mobilised, as needed. Mentoring involves 'coaching, cajoling and character building' and is provided in one-to-one private sessions or in small groups.

Students' Voices:

- *'When I arrived at the college, I was given a test which helped me find the areas I was good at and some I had weaknesses in. I went to the study workshop and drew up an action plan which I am now working through.'*
- *'The college has lent me a spell-checker and I get a lot of help and advice which is helping me to understand how to cope with my dyslexia. I never knew before what was causing me so many problems.'*

Good Practice in Action

Characteristic Five

Financial and practical support is provided

Needs of learner	Role of provider	Standards for colleges	Evidence
help with fees, travel costs, financial emergencies, costs of textbooks, equipment, examination fees	provide hardship funds, use access funds fairly, make links with educational charities and other external funding devise policies on the purchase of text books, waiving of fees, payment of examination fees	financial and practical support is jointly planned with learners from under-represented groups; good use is made of available resources; effectiveness of financial practical support is reviewed	records show use of access funds, applications to charities etc. relevant policies
help with childcare or costs of child-minding	provide childcare facilities or a childcare allowance make use of existing community-based childcare	reasons for learners from underrepresented groups not completing or progressing are sought and analysed	numbers of learners from underrepresented groups assisted through childcare arrangements/ funds evaluations of support arrangements
opportunities to discuss problems relating to their studies and to agree strategies for overcoming them	with learners draw up plans to overcome practical difficulties preventing or hindering study	support is provided to encourage these learners to return to study	summaries of reasons for leaving of non-completers and records of action taken to support these learners records of interviews with learners resulting in action plans

Key Recommendations:

- colleges should identify the range of practical support each learner needs and plan with them how to meet these needs
- there should be clear criteria for allocating practical assistance to all learners; funding should be prioritised for those learners who have greatest needs
- information about practical support should be given to all learners, including those in outreach centres
- colleges should assess the benefits of providing practical support for learners and the effects in any areas where they are not providing support.

Case Studies

Examples of Good Practice

Free transport
Reaseheath College, in partnership with Cheshire County Council, helps learners travel to the college. There is a wide-ranging service within the county and some out-of-county learners can be provided with a free bus-pass. College staff also act as advocates for learners who have been refused assistance with travel by local authorities: they help with appeals, contact local councillors and local authority officers and have been successful in getting assistance for individuals. Almost a third of all full-time learners benefit from the scheme.

Partnership to support childcare
At West Kent College learners on a basic skills course at an outreach centre are able to attend because the college has negotiated free childcare arrangements with social services. The nursery is on the same premises as the classes. Courses are linked to child development; for example, learners produce books which are used by the children in the nursery.

Comprehensive childcare support
Newham Women's Training and Education Centre learners are entitled to childcare support. Parents can choose to bring their children to the centre's nursery, or use a social services registered childminder, and for their older children at school up to the age of 12 to be collected and looked after by childminders. In response to learners who preferred their children to be looked after by someone from their own cultural background, the centre jointly set up courses with social services to train women from minority ethnic groups to become childminders.

The positive impact of financial support
'Fast Forward' is a Nottinghamshire County Council initiative which includes college partners, and is designed to encourage and support adults who are unemployed or on low incomes to participate in education and training and progress onto employment. The project provides a maximum of £100 for travel and childcare costs, some course fees and individual support for materials such as uniforms, tools or essential visits. 'Fast Forward' is for learners living within the area whether they study in Nottinghamshire or elsewhere. Since 1992, over 6,000 learners have received support. College data show that the success rate of these learners on courses averages 90 per cent.

Students' Voices:

- *'I would not have been able to come to college for the catering course at all if the college hadn't helped me to buy my knives: they cost nearly £100.'*
- *'My daughter loves the crèche here and it means I can attend the GNVQ in graphic design.'*

Good Practice in Action

Characteristic Six

There is an appropriate and relevant curriculum which enables students to progress

Needs of learner	Role of provider	Standards for colleges	Evidence
a curriculum which allows different entry points and levels of study	devise a curriculum plan focusing on the needs of underrepresented groups	clear rationale for programmes offered to underrepresented groups	curriculum policy and plan which includes a focus on the curriculum for learners from under-represented groups
content relevant to the needs and interests of underrepresented groups	provide a number of entry points within a year, a choice of levels and progression routes, and introduce modular provision	programmes planned and reviewed specifically to meet the learning needs of targeted learners	programmes plans and schemes of work which demonstrate relevance of curriculum to target group
a curriculum which allows development at learners' own pace	support the introduction of new assessment strategies and appropriate staff-development activities	flexible programmes of study with suitable assessment methods	assessment policy for programmes for learners from underrepresented groups
suitable assessment methods and supportive feedback preparation for progression opportunities	provide different modes and times of study create enrichment opportunities		records of assessment feedback records of enrichment activities

Key Recommendations:

- colleges need to review and develop their programmes regularly to ensure that they meet the needs of underrepresented groups
- flexible programmes of study and non-threatening methods of assessment are essential to recruiting and retaining learners from underrepresented groups
- entry to study should not be limited to one time in the year and courses should not necessarily be timed traditionally
- education for learners from underrepresented groups needs to be broadened by enrichment activities.

Case Studies

Examples of Good Practice

Bespoke courses
Ruskin College's close links with trade unions and community organisations are used to develop new courses and adapt existing ones to meet needs. The college runs various short courses designed specifically for community groups, for example, social work skills and cultural awareness for the 'Refugees in Oxford' community organisation. Many of these bespoke courses also generate up-to-date case study material which the college also uses for teaching on other courses.

Courses designed to meet the needs of deaf learners
The City Literary Institute designed a programme to meet the needs and interests of deaf learners. Learners can study a core programme which includes English, English for speakers of other languages, mathematics and communications such as British Sign Language, lip-reading and communication with deaf-blind people. In addition, learners can join other courses at the Institute, further education colleges and universities across London, and receive specialist support provided by the Institute.

The Connections programme
Norwich City College of Further and Higher Education's Connections programme provides an accessible and flexible modular curriculum both in college and in community venues. The programme has a range of personal development modules and vocational 'taster' modules. It is timetabled to fit in with school hours and learners can study full time or part time. Continual assessment procedures replace traditional tests and examinations. There are two levels to the programme and two points of entry.

Using technology to provide a flexible curriculum
Weymouth College identified in its rural catchment area, which had high levels of unemployment, that adult learners required open and flexible study routes to qualifications. The curriculum is delivered using new technology and distance learning methods. The programme combines assessment and accreditation of learners' prior learning and experience, psychometric testing, workshops, tutorials, optional short courses, technology-based training and distance learning. There are also work placement and workplace projects, an employer information service and provision for exit guidance.

Students' Voices:

- *'A representative from the college came out to assess what the company needed, and has devised a programme which suits exactly what we need people to be able to do. The bonus is that they have also arranged for our workers to get a qualification.'*
- *'It never occurred to me that I could go to college: I'm so tied to the house. But I learned about open learning from a poster in the local library and though I don't think I actually could do it alone, in fact, we have a study group which meets there every week and I have a tutor who I can ring up and have a chat to.'*

Good Practice in Action

Characteristic Seven

There is effective teaching and learning

Needs of learner	Role of provider	Standards for colleges	Evidence
Teaching which: is pitched at the right level and is differentiated to meet individual needs values learners' prior experience develops confidence builds knowledge and skills at a suitable pace pays attention to key skills provides supportive feedback motivates through encouragement, interest and the relevance of content to learners' aims	develop teachers' skills exchange good practice integrate key skill development with other studies ensure that course review and evaluation has a strong focus on teaching and learning provide the best possible resources, accommodation and technician support develop the use of information technology for teaching and learning develop open, distance and flexible learning	appropriately qualified teachers regular sharing of expertise in working with underrepresented groups staff development is encouraged targeted programmes include systematic development of key skills the quality of teaching is rated at least as highly by targeted learners as others information technology is used to support teaching and learning open, distance and flexible learning modes are available	records of staff development and team meetings schemes of work and lesson plans course review documents college's self-assessment of teaching based on lesson observations evaluation of the quality of teaching by learners from underrepresented groups records of visits by external verifiers and moderators

Key Recommendations:

- the teaching for learners from underrepresented groups must be undertaken by appropriately qualified staff supported by development activities and opportunities to learn from each other
- programmes of study should develop key skills, build confidence and if needed be differentiated by activity and outcome
- resource allocation must ensure the same levels of support for these programmes as other programmes
- the use of information technology, open, distance and flexible learning need to be developed and sustained.

Case Studies

Examples of Good Practice

Overcoming negative experiences of learning
Most learners on the Women's Technology Training Ltd in Liverpool left school with few or no qualifications and a sense of failure. Teachers work hard to help them overcome the negative views they have of themselves. From the start of courses, learners are introduced to the idea that 'if you don't understand something it is the staff's fault not yours.' Teachers develop and exchange ideas and use practical exercises which are fun and relieve learners' anxieties without being patronising.

Choosing how to learn
At Dearne Valley College flexi-study arrangements and open workshops help those who cannot or prefer not to attend regular classes. Learning methods and times are adjusted to suit learners' needs. The flexi-study scheme is tutor-supported self-study. Tutorials can be at home, in college, individually, in pairs or in groups. The open workshops are described as 'drop in, pay as you go'. Learners buy a book of tickets for £1.00 an hour to attend the workshop and use open learning packages when it suits them. An individual learning agreement is drawn up with each learner and their learning is closely monitored.

Using new technology
The Rural Vocational Training Project is run jointly by Northumberland TEC, the Rural Development Council and Derwentside College. People in remote rural areas who have a suitable computer are provided with a modem so that they can access distance learning packages supported by an on-line graphical bulletin board. Learners include those from small and medium size enterprises, the housebound and disabled. Tutorial support is also delivered electronically through telematics, the use of fax, telephone, voice-mail and electronic mail.

Improving the quality of teaching through classroom observations
Fircroft College of Adult Education teachers use lesson observation to focus on the cultural diversity of materials used in courses and to evaluate learners' interaction in relation to sex and race. Teachers analyse findings from classroom observations to check that male and female learners and learners from different minority ethnic groups are given equal amounts of attention from teachers, and that teaching is effective for all learners.

Students' Voices:

- *'I thought that college would be just like school us all sitting in desks in rows and never saying a word. But it's not like that – we work a lot in groups, and are able to listen and talk to each other it's amazing what I've learned from other people.'*
- *'I like the way the teachers are like friends: they treat us with respect and discuss with us how we would like to approach certain topics. I've been able to do my English language project on my own daughter's development of language.'*

Good Practice in Action

Characteristic Eight

There are mechanisms for recording students' achievements which: acknowledge all learning, are meaningful to students and are recognised by employers, education providers and others

Needs of learner	Role of provider	Standards for colleges	Evidence
help in understanding the framework of awards on offer and their currency support in identifying previous achievements and to build upon them to have achievements recognised at stages throughout the period of study	select appropriate methods of accreditation and award which record small steps, allow transfer of credits, assess, accredit and build upon prior learning and are validated by external organisations enable the development of modular programmes develop systems which demonstrate value added ensure guidance staff are well briefed on all awards to inform employers of the value of all achievements	targeted learners use accreditation of previous learning there are systems to record and recognise small steps in learning learners understand how to achieve credits and qualifications targeted learners complete courses and achieve qualifications at least as well as others learners' achievements are celebrated	the framework of accreditation and awards used for targeted learners individual records of achievement kept by these learners records of accreditation of prior learning for these learners overall achievements of these learners added value analysis for these learners learners' views on the forms of accreditation used records of events to celebrate achievements

Key Recommendations:

- accreditation must allow for the recognition of small steps in achievement and for credit to be transferred
- systematic measurement of analysis of value added among targeted learners needs to be undertaken
- awards should be well understood by staff and learners alike and their achievement celebrated.

Case Studies

Examples of Good Practice

Credit passports

Open College Networks (OCN) issue learners with an official Credit Record which records the number of credits they gain at different levels and the titles of all units achieved. If learners move onto other OCN accredited courses, further credits gained can be added to the Credit Record. National OCN partnership arrangements may also enable learners to transfer credits towards qualifications offered by other awarding bodies. Learners, particularly those who have not received any formal recognition of their achievements in the past, value the way the Credit Record gives recognition to each 'small step' or unit of their learning. It boosts their confidence, makes them feel proud of their achievements and often helps to spur them onto study further to accumulate more credits.

Learning outcomes on non-accredited courses

The Workers' Educational Association, in partnership with other designated colleges, has explored and developed ways of assessing and valuing learners' learning on non-accredited courses. Teachers write plans for courses which identify the intended outcomes and learners are able to negotiate their own outcomes thus courses reflect the requirements of learners. During the course, teachers involve learners in assessing to what extent they have achieved the learning outcomes agreed, to identify other learning achievements and to suggest what courses to study next.

Learning management

The recording of achievement system in Loughborough College has been used to tackle the difficulties learners face in learning. It is well supported by a training programme for personal tutors, now called learning tutors, who use a review and action planning cycle to help learners to progress in their work. Tutorial time has become 'learning management time'. The outcome has been to move learners towards taking responsibility for planning their own learning. They are more able to meet deadlines and complete assignments. They are able to achieve additional accreditation through evidence collected while on work experience placement and during learning management time.

Celebrating learners' achievements

Evesham College has an annual special awards ceremony that recognises outstanding progress, effort and achievement. The occasion is jointly sponsored by 26 local firms. The college celebrates notable successes of its learners in group or individual achievement. Several learners who started courses with little confidence and low levels of skills have had their individual progress recognised and received awards. It also recognises achievement in enrichment activities.

Students' Voices:

- *'I like to be able to get confirmation of what I have achieved quickly and that means I can plan my next step.'*
- *'By reviewing what I am good at with my tutor I can then see what things I have to work harder at.'*

Good Practice in Action

Characteristic Nine

Management information is accurate and used to evaluate students' progress and other aspects of provision

Needs of learner	Role of provider	Standards for colleges	Evidence
information on how well other learners have done on similar programmes, and the opportunities that have been open to them as a result information on individual progress	develop systems which collect accurate data and analyse them in formats which contribute to effective monitoring, evaluation and planning use learners' achievement data to publicise learning opportunities make correlations between improved retention, and attendance rates and achievements and the quality of learners' experiences use management information to improve the quality of provision	systems monitor rates of participation, satisfaction, retention, achievement and progress for different learner groups data are used to evaluate success of targeted learners in enrolment, completion, achievements and progress comparisons of the performance of these learners to others locally and nationally there is analysis of learners from under-represented groups who leave early or who are unsuccessful identification of additional data needed	data summarising numbers of learners from underrepresented groups enrolled at the college analysis of which courses are chosen by learners from target groups, and why data summarising enrolment rates, satisfaction rates, retention rates, achievement rates and destinations of these learners report analysing the data and evaluating the college's success in meeting the needs of these learners report comparing the performance of these learners with those of others

Key Recommendations:

- colleges should use management information to support, record and assess learners' progress as individuals and in groups
- colleges should examine the correlation between attendance, retention rates, achievements and learners' backgrounds
- colleges should analyse whether particular groups are underrepresented or overrepresented in some curriculum areas and levels of study.

Case Studies

Examples of Good Practice

A tailored system of collecting accurate data
Runshaw College has developed its own management information system tailored to identified needs. The detail and accuracy of the information allows a quick response to support a learner who is having difficulties and to identify and address problems on courses. If there are difficulties in particular courses then lesson observation and staff development activities take place to plan corrective action. The system has helped the college in improving its attendance and retention rates and achievements.

Learner tracking
Hackney Community College tracks all learners by using their unique student number. Tracking has helped the college to support learners and to plan the curriculum. College data show that 14 per cent of learners on non-schedule two courses in 1995-96 progressed to schedule two courses in 1996-97. Approximately a quarter of learners progressed from one non-schedule 2 course to another. This latter finding supports other research which suggests some learners may take several years of undertaking non-schedule 2 courses before they progress to schedule two courses.

Retention improvement at outreach centres
A project to improve learner retention in North Warwickshire and Hinckley College's outreach centres is based on computerised learner tracking linked to learner support. In all outreach centres absence is monitored through the direct inputting of data. The project is underpinned by learner agreements which set out the learner's attendance responsibilities, learning agreements which provide a regular check on progress, and a responsive learner support system.

Using data to meet needs
Canterbury College's data highlighted a problem in attracting learners from the Isle of Sheppey due to the long distance learners had to travel and the rather isolated nature of communities on the island. Research was undertaken with over 400 Sheppey residents identifying training needs and courses were established in a purpose built centre on Sheppey in response to these needs. The college carefully tracks the success of these learners. It knows that learners who start on courses at levels one or two on Sheppey often progress onto level three courses at the college, so it has supported them in obtaining cheap travel to the college.

Students' Voices:

- *'I came back to enrol on a course this year and the college had all my details on their computer.'*
- *'One thing that attracted me to the college was that they sent us details about how people who had left our school had done at college. Nearly all of them had got qualifications and a lot had got jobs or places on higher level courses. I thought, if they could do it, so could I.'*

Appendices

Appendix one

How the characteristics of good practice were formulated

In developing the characteristics we:

- used evidence from different groups with an interest and/or responsibility for further education, including students, teachers, managers, policy-makers, and from groups who do not usually participate in further education
- tested characteristics of good practice in widening participation through visits to 40 colleges and developed them as effective tools for auditing and improving strategies for widening participation
- identified effective practice in widening participation developed by the different providers of further and adult education across England
- drew on the findings of relevant published reports to find key messages applicable to widening participation across the further education sector
- analysed and interpreted the wealth of statistical data collected by the Council about students' backgrounds, their achievements and destinations.

We would like to thank all those colleges who gave so freely of their time to help inspectors gather the evidence required. All of this work was expertly guided by the Widening Participation Committee's Quality and Performance task group, whose members included colleagues from NIACE, FEDA, UCAS, further education colleges and higher education. A team seconded from the FEFC inspectorate carried out the research and analysis.

Appendix two

A summary of additional inspection findings

The inspectorate found many examples of good practice on their visits to colleges. It has been impossible to include them all in this guide. Some other colleges involved in interesting work in widening participation are listed below for information.

Characteristic One – Marketing which is planned and based on intelligence

East Durham Community College: use of community workers to identify needs

Gateshead College: comprehensive initial market research for the Learning World Centre

North Tyneside College: use of local radio

Characteristic Two – Strategies for contacting non-participants

Coventry Technical College: community advisory panel

Hull College: partnerships with primary schools

Manchester College of Arts and Technology: working with inner city schools

Plater College: using parish networks

Plymouth College of Further Education: courses for school age mothers

Sheffield College: working with different minority ethnic communities to set up literacy campaigns

Teesside Tertiary College: classes in unusual venues

Trowbridge College: establishing community colleges

Varndean College: working with Sudanese refugees

Wakefield College, Halesown College, Coalville Technical College and Doncaster College: working with travellers

Characteristic Three – Good-quality information and guidance which is readily available and impartial

Hackney Community College: progression route mapping and training of adult education tutors

Middlesbrough College: 'flying' tutors visit adult education classes

Characteristic Four – Effective support for learning

Halton College: video conferencing

Kingsway College: support for learners with learning difficulties and/or disabilities

Tower Hamlets College: supporting learners from minority ethnic groups

Characteristic Five – Provision of financial and practical support

Gloucestershire College of Arts and Technology: support for learners who care for elderly or housebound relatives

Oldham College: women only and mature learners' common rooms

Richmond Adult and Community College: supplementary access funds

Characteristic Six – An appropriate and relevant curriculum which enables students to progress

Amersham and Wycombe College: tailor-made programmes of learning

Bournville College of Further Education: attracting reluctant learners

Bury College: fast track GNVQs

Charles Keene College: family literacy at the Linwood Centre

City and Islington College: GCE A level subjects modularised for Access learners

Fareham College: mixing modules from different courses

Melton Mowbray College: work with unemployed women in rural areas

Otley College of Agriculture and Horticulture: curriculum relevance through modularisation

Tile Hill College of Further Education: literacy and numeracy through the youth service

Characteristic Seven – Effective teaching and learning

Blackburn College: use of cable television

Clarendon College, Nottingham: training staff from partner organisations in teaching and curriculum management

Dudley College of Technology: bilingual teaching

Exeter College: the work of the adult basic skills unit

Morley College: Access learners identify their preferred learning styles.

Reaseheath College: training for teachers working with foundation level learners

Characteristic Eight – There are mechanisms for recording students' achievements which acknowledge all learning, are meaningful to students and are recognised by employers, education providers and others

City of Bath College: recording module and unit achievements

NEW College, Pontefract: use of 'value added' analysis to raise learners' expectations of achievement

Characteristic Nine – Management information which is accurate and used to evaluate students' progress and other aspects of provision

Hillcroft College: analysing examination results by ethnicity

Newcastle College: attendance and progress tracking

Appendix three

Bibliography

Learning Works: Widening participation in further education, Helena Kennedy QC, The Further Education Funding Council, Coventry, 1997

Inclusive Learning: Report of the Learning Difficulties and/or Disabilities Committee, The Further Education Funding Council, HMSO, London, 1996

Identifying and Addressing Needs: A practical guide, Institute for Employment Studies, The Further Education Funding Council, Coventry, 1997

Marketing Case Studies in Further Education Colleges, Pieda PLC, Department for Education and Employment, Sheffield, 1996

Towards Self-assessing Colleges, Stella Dixon, FE Matters: Volume 1 Number 4, Further Education Development Agency, London, 1996

Creating Connections: College innovations in flexibility, access and participation, Further Education Development Agency, Association of Colleges, Blagdon, 1996

Pragmatic Prospects: Developing LEA adult education, edited by Bob Powell and Pablo Foster, Further Education Development Agency, Blagdon, 1996

Student Retention: Case studies of strategies that work, Paul Martinez, FE Matters Volume 1 Number 6, Further Education Development Agency, Blagdon, 1996

Transforming Teaching: Selecting and evaluating teaching strategies, Carole Mitchell, FE Matters: Volume 1 Number 14, Further Education Development Agency, Blagdon, 1997

On Course for Next Steps: Careers education and guidance for students in FE, Jackie Sadler and Anna Reisenberger, Developing FE: Volume 1 Number 5, Further Education Development Agency, London, 1997

Adult Learners: Pathways to progression, Anna Reisenberger and John Sanders, FE Matters: Volume 1 Number 12, Further Education Development Agency, Blagdon, 1997

Adults with Learning Difficulties: Education for choice & empowerment: A handbook of good practice, Jeannie Sutcliffe, National Institute of Adult Continuing Education, Open University, Leicester, 1990

Education's for Other People: Access to education for non-participant adults, Veronica McGivney, National Institute of Adult Continuing Education, Leicester, 1990

Educational Guidance with Black Communities, Stella Dadzie, National Institute of Adult Continuing Education, Leicester, 1990

Enabling Learning: A student-centred approach to teaching adults with learning difficulties, Jeannie Sutcliffe, National Institute of Adult Continuing Education, Leicester, 1996

Engaging with Difference: The 'other' in adult education, edited by Mary Stuart and Alastair Thomson, National Institute of Adult Continuing Education, Leicester, 1995

Learning for a Purpose: Participation in education and training by adults from ethnic minorities, Naomi Sargant, National Institute of Adult Continuing Education, Leicester, 1993

Motivating Unemployed Adults to Undertake Education and Training: Some British and other European findings, Veronica McGivney, National Institute of Adult Continuing Education, Leicester, 1992

Staying or Leaving the Course: Non-completion and retention of mature students in further and higher education, Veronica McGivney, National Institute of Adult Continuing Education, Leicester, 1996

The Learning Divide: A study of participation in adult learning in the United Kingdom, Naomi Sargant, John Field, Hywel Francis, Tom Schuller and Alan Tuckett, National Institute of Adult Continuing Education, Leicester, 1997

Towards Inclusion: Developing integrated education for adults with learning difficulties, Jeannie Sutcliffe, National Institute of Adult Continuing Education, Leicester, 1996

Widening Participation: Routes to a learning society: A policy discussion paper, Tony Uden, National Institute of Adult Continuing Education, Leicester, 1996

Women, Education and Training, Veronica McGivney, National Institute of Adult Continuing Education, Leicester, 1993

Working with Black Adult Learners, Stella Dadzie, National Institute of Adult Continuing Education, Leicester, 1993

The Basic Skills of Young Adults: Some findings from the 1970 British Cohort Study, Carol Ekinsmyth and John Bynner, Adult Literacy and Basic Skills Unit, London, 1994

Older and Younger: The basic skills of different age groups, Adult Literacy and Basic Skills Unit, London, 1995

Difficulties with Basic Skills: Findings from the 1970 British Cohort Study, John Bynner and Jane Steedman, Basic Skills Agency, London, 1995

Where next? Drop out and progression from ESOL provision, Maria Kambouri, Inji Toutounji and Hazel Francis, Basic Skills Agency, London, 1996

Lost Opportunities: The language skills of linguistic minorities in England and Wales, Roy Carr-Hill, Steve Passingham, Alison Wolf and Naomi Kent, Basic Skills Agency, London, 1996

Assessing Reading, Writing and Maths, Basic Skills Agency, London, 1996

Basic Skills Support: A guide for every teacher, Sue Silk, Basic Skills Agency, London, 1994

Open Learning and ESOL, Liz Voss, Basic Skills Agency, London, 1991

Appendix 4

Measuring Widening Participation

The National Baseline 1994-95 to 1995-96

Introduction

How to Widen Participation: A Guide to Good Practice describes the framework developed by the Widening Participation Committee to enable colleges and other providers to set targets and measure their performance in widening participation.

The information in this annex provides a national picture of further education students in 1994-95 and 1995-96, using the factors described in the framework, for providers at local level to use as comparators.

It is expected that the information will be updated annually and published as a statistical bulletin, to show what progress has been made at national level in widening participation in further education. Colleges and other providers are invited to send any comments on the content and layout of the annex, which can be taken into account in the annual updates, to:

The Research and Statistics Team
Further Education Funding Council
Cheylesmore House
Quinton Road
Coventry CV1 2WT

Content

The framework covers student recruitment, retention, achievement and progression. The tables illustrate how the framework can be used to set a baseline from which progress can be measured. Each table is accompanied by a brief commentary explaining how the information can be used locally.

The results shown in this annex relate to students enrolled in further education colleges in England in the 1994-95 and 1995-96 teaching years. Data are derived from the individualised student record (ISR) returns made by colleges to the Council. A separate volume: *Widening Participation in Further Education: Statistical Evidence* (to be published in autumn 1997) explains in greater detail the methodology underlying the statistics.

Recruitment

Participation rates of the percentage of the population enrolled at further education colleges can be calculated by dividing numbers recruited by numbers in the population. Table 1 shows participation rates in further education by type of college, broad mode of attendance and by age group. Locally, individual colleges can use their own student data to calculate their participation rate (also known as penetration rate) into the local community. Or, by combining information with other colleges and providers, they can calculate a participation rate in their area to compare with the national rates. As well as a breakdown by age group, participation rates can be calculated by other characteristics such as by sex (table 2) or by ethnic group (table 3).

Table 1 includes participants who are enrolled at further education colleges but not with other providers such as schools, or private providers funded by training and enterprise councils (TECs). Colleges can obtain a more comprehensive picture of local participation by combining data with other local providers.

Sex and ethnicity profiles

Tables 2 and 3 show the sex and ethnicity distribution respectively of students in further education colleges by age group compared to the population as a whole. Colleges can calculate the distribution of their own students to compare with local population statistics.

Nationally colleges recruit a higher proportion of female than male students. Younger students are evenly distributed between the sexes, but there are significantly more female than male students among older age groups. For example 60 per cent of 40 to 49 year old students are female, whereas in the population as a whole there is a 50:50 split between the sexes in this age group.

The ethnicity profile shows that nationally further education colleges are recruiting a higher proportion of students from ethnic minorities than the percentage in the population generally. There are, however, significant local variations. For colleges with a significant ethnic minority population in their local area it would be appropriate to disaggregate this table further by sex as well as by age group and to look in detail at the recruitment of individual minority ethnic groups.

Level of qualification

Table 4 shows the national distribution of students by age group according to the notional level of qualification they are studying for. At local level, this table could be broken down further, for example by sex and by ethnic group to monitor whether students from different ethnic minority groups are recruited onto particular types of qualifications or levels of study.

Nationally, over half of 16 to 18 year old students are studying at level 3, with a quarter studying at level 2. In 1995-96, around a quarter of adult students were studying qualifications at entry level or level 1.

Prior attainment by age group

Table 5 provides details of qualifications on entry for 16 and 17 year old students in 1995-96, in the form of a points score. The information is for a sample of 176 colleges: 82 sixth form colleges and 94 other further education colleges, for which sufficient data on students' prior attainments were recorded on the ISR in 1995-96. The notes below the table explain how the points score was calculated for each student.

Locally, colleges can compare the profile of students' achievements on entering the institution, with the national picture, to see what types of students they are recruiting and to monitor the effect of recruitment campaigns, for example to recruit young people with low levels of prior attainment.

Nationally the profile of young people recruited by sixth form colleges is significantly different from other colleges, with 72 per cent of 16 year olds in sixth form colleges in 1995 96 having reached foundation target 1 (five GCSEs at grades A to C) when they were recruited. In other further education colleges, 44 per cent of 16 year olds have reached foundation target on entry to the institution and another 26 per cent have achieved 30 or more points in their GCSEs. Nationally, about 45 per cent of young people complete their compulsory schooling having obtained foundation target 1.

A higher percentage of female students than male students enrolled in colleges have reached foundation target 1. This is particular marked for 16 year olds in further education and tertiary colleges.

In 1994-95 and 1995-96 it was not compulsory for colleges to record the prior attainments of their students on the ISR. In fact, a sample of colleges did record qualifications on entry, and this information has been used to produce table 5. From 1996-97 onwards, when recording prior attainment became compulsory for students on Council-funded provision, it should be possible to extend the analysis shown here to include retention and achievement rates by level of previous qualification.

Adult students receiving benefit

Tables 6 to 9 show the percentage of adult students aged 19 and over in receipt of benefit and their characteristics. The notes below table 9 explain how to identify these students from the ISR.

Colleges can use this kind of information to identify the socio-economic characteristics of adult students where qualifications on entry are not available and to monitor the effect of recruitment campaigns. The numbers of students on benefit will vary substantially between colleges depending on local circumstances. Locally, data on benefits or unemployment rates would provide a helpful context to college data.

Nationally:

- almost a fifth of adult students in colleges are in receipt of benefit or are dependent on someone receiving benefit. A similar proportion of male and female students are receiving benefit (table 6)
- those students who do study whilst on benefit are more likely to be aged between 20 and 40 where the percentage on benefits is highest (table 7)
- almost half of black African adults are on benefit compared to less than a fifth of white and Chinese adult students. Black Caribbean and black other ethnic groups also have high percentages of students on benefits (table 8)
- students on benefit are studying for qualifications at all levels although there are more on level 2 courses studying for GCSEs or NVQs and fewer studying for higher level qualifications than compared to the total adult student population (table 9).

Postcodes

Table 10 shows the distribution of students recruited by colleges in 1994-95 from areas with different social and economic characteristics and compares this with England as a whole. 1995-96 data was not fully available when the research was carried out for the committee.

Postcodes are used to determine which local authority ward the student resides in. An index of local conditions developed by the Department of the Environment (DoE) which measures relative levels of deprivation across all wards in England, provides a score for the deprivation in each ward. The index comprises seven socio-economic factors taken from the 1991 national population census. Further details are set out in *Widening Participation in Further Education: Statistical Evidence*.

Locally, colleges can use this method to identify the socio-economic characteristics of students and to monitor the effect of recruitment campaigns. The DoE index of local conditions is also available at enumeration district (ED) level and can be obtained from Keith Solwell at the London Research Centre on 0171 787 5658. Colleges can request the information for a number of local authority 1991 districts. The index is then provided for all the wards or EDs in those districts. An administrative charge is payable depending on the amount of data requested. The minimum is £40.

The distribution of wards with high levels of deprivation varies considerably between different parts of the country, with inner city areas generally showing much higher numbers of wards with high levels of deprivation than other areas. Other factors or indexes can be used as an alternative to the DoE index. For example, unemployment rates also provide a measure of deprivation.

Nationally, further education colleges recruit a higher percentage of their students from deprived areas than the distribution of deprived wards in

England generally. A greater percentage of adult students are recruited from very deprived areas than 16 to 18 year old students.

Retention

Tables 11 to 14 show in-year retention rates for students by different characteristics such as age and sex (table 11), age and ethnic group (table 12), level of qualification being studied (table 13), economic status of adult students (table 14). In-year retention measures whether students complete or continue their studies within the teaching year or if they withdraw from all their qualifications. Short courses of less than 12 weeks in length are not included.

The tables show retention in the 1994-95 teaching year. 1995-96 data was not available when research into retention rates was carried out for the committee. The retention rates shown here include a wider group of students than those included in the published performance indicators for colleges relating to continuation. Further details are given in the notes to the tables.

Analysis of ISR data has shown there are certain groups of students that once recruited are more difficult to retain than other students and whose achievement rates are lower. In order to widen participation, colleges need to ensure that students of all types complete their learning programmes and go on to achieve the qualifications they are studying for.

Nationally:

- 88 per cent of males and 90 per cent of females studying full time were retained on their programmes of study in 1994-95. Males and females studying part time have similar retention rates. Adults aged 25 and over studying part time have the highest retention rates. Part-time 16 to 18 year olds appear to be the hardest to retain
- retention rates of students from different ethnic groups vary greatly, particularly for the 16 to 18 age group. Black Caribbean and black other students of all ages are harder to retain than other students, particularly Chinese and Indian students who have the lowest withdrawal rates. This is linked to the high proportion of black ethnic minority students on benefit, which is associated with lower retention
- on average, students studying for qualifications at notional level 3 and 4 have higher retention rates than those studying at levels 1 and 2
- adult students on benefits have lower retention rates than other adult students.

Achievement

Tables 15 to 18 show achievement rates for students by different characteristics such as age and sex (table 15), ethnic group (table 16), level of qualification being studied for (table 17), and economic status of adult students (table 18). The tables show achievement rates in the 1994-95 teaching year. 1995-96 data was not available when research into achievement rates was carried out for the committee.

Achievement rates have been calculated only for students completing the final year of their studies, as measured from the ISR by the expected end-dates of their qualifications. Students who withdraw from the college before the end of their studies are not included in the calculation. The achievement rates shown here are calculated in a different way to the published performance indicator for colleges relating to achievement. Further details are given in the notes to the tables.

As stated above, analysis of ISR data has shown there are certain groups of students that once recruited are more difficult to retain than other students and whose achievement rates are lower. In order to widen participation colleges need to ensure that students of all types complete their qualifications and go on to achieve the qualifications they are studying for.

Locally, colleges will wish to take account of previously published analysis from the ISR which has shown that on average achievement rates are higher in specialist colleges and sixth form colleges than in other types of college.

Nationally:

- female students studying full time have higher rates of achievements than males studying full time at 81 per cent and 75 per cent respectively including partial achievement. Achievement rates for part time students are similar for female and male students but show a different pattern of full and partial achievement. This is likely to be because full-time students tend to study for more than one qualification. Of they achieve some but not all of their qualifications they are shown as a partially achieving student
- achievement rates of students from different ethnic groups vary significantly. As with retention rates, black African and black Caribbean students have lower achievement rates compared to other ethnic groups. Again, this is linked to the high proportion of black ethnic minority students on benefit, which is associated with lower achievement. White and Bangladeshi students tend to have higher achievement rates
- on average, achievement rates on NVQs and GNVQs are lower than for other types of qualifications. Highest achievement rates are for GCE A levels being studied fulltime and GNVQ precursors at level 3
- adult students on benefits have lower achievement rates than other adult students.

Progression and destinations

Table 19 shows the destinations of students completing their studies in 1994-95. Four types of destinations are recorded in the ISR: further education, higher education, employment and other. In 1994-95 destinations were unknown for over half of full-time students and three quarters of part-time students.

Some 37 per cent of full-time students where the destination was known continued in further education, 32 per cent entered higher education and 24 per cent were in employment. For those part-time students whose destinations had been recorded 48 per cent continued in further education, 4 per cent went on to higher education and 41 per cent were in employment. This includes both those students continuing in their current employment and those entering new employment.

Locally, progression and destinations could be monitored in more detail by disaggregating table 19 by age group, sex, ethnic group or level of qualification.

Abbreviations used in the tables

The following abbreviations are used in the tables:

FE	further education
M	male
F	female
FT	full-time
PT	part-time.

Recruitment: age, sex

Table 1. Participation rates (%) of students in FE colleges 1995-96 by mode of attendance and by age

	College type							
	general FE and tertiary		sixth form		other		all colleges	
Age group	FT	PT	FT	PT	FT	PT	FT	PT
under 16	~	0.4	~	~	~	~	~	0.5
16-18	21.7	11.2	6.7	0.3	0.7	0.5	29.1	12.0
19-59	1.0	8.2	~	0.2	~	0.2	1.0	8.6
60 and over	~	1.7	~	~	~	~	~	1.8
Overall participation rate	**1.3**	**5.4**	**0.2**	**0.2**	**~**	**0.1**	**1.6**	**5.7**

~ less than 0.1%

Source: individualised student record (ISR) July 1996, 1995-96; Office of National Statistics population estimates

Coverage: figures grossed up for all colleges from 327 colleges; includes Council and non-Council funded provision

Table 2. Students' sex profile (%) by age compared to the population

Age group	1994-95		1995-96		Population profile	
	F	M	F	M	F	M
under 16	51	49	50	50	49	51
16	49	51	50	50	49	51
17	49	51	50	50	48	52
18	46	54	47	53	48	52
19	46	54	48	52	49	51
20	49	51	50	50	49	51
21-24	55	45	55	45	49	51
25-29	56	44	55	45	49	51
30-39	59	41	58	42	49	51
40-49	62	38	60	40	50	50
50-59	57	43	57	43	50	50
60+	59	41	60	40	57	43
All ages	**55**	**45**	**55**	**45**	**51**	**49**

Source: individualised student record (ISR) 1994-95 and 1995-96; Office of National Statistics mid-1995 population estimates

Coverage: 1994-95; 373 colleges, 1995-96; 413 colleges; includes Council and non-Council funded provision

Recruitment: ethnicity, notional level

Table 3. Students' ethnicity profile (%) by age group compared to the population

	under 16		16-19		20 and over		all age groups		
Ethnicity	students 1994-95	population	students 1994-95	population	students 1994-95	population	students 1994-95	students 1995-96	population
Bangladeshi	0.9	0.8	1.4	0.6	0.9	0.2	1.1	0.7	0.3
Black African	0.7	0.6	1.2	0.5	1.7	0.4	1.5	1.5	0.4
Black Carribean	1.7	1.2	1.7	1.0	2.5	1.0	2.2	2.0	1.1
Black other	0.7	0.9	0.8	0.5	0.7	0.2	0.7	0.6	0.4
Chinese	0.4	0.3	0.6	0.4	0.5	0.3	0.5	0.5	0.3
Indian	6.4	2.6	3.3	2.2	1.9	1.5	2.4	2.4	1.8
Pakistani	3.8	2.0	3.0	1.5	1.9	0.6	2.3	2.0	1.0
White	82.6	89.8	86.0	92.2	86.7	95.0	86.4	87.6	93.8
Other - Asian	0.5	0.5	0.4	0.4	0.7	0.4	0.6	0.8	0.4
Other	2.2	1.2	1.6	0.7	2.5	0.4	2.2	1.8	0.6
Total	**100**	**100**	**100**	**100**	**100**	**100**	**100**	**100**	**100**

Source: individualised student record (ISR) 1994-95 and 1995-96; 1991 population census

Coverage: 1994-95; 373 colleges, 1995-96; 413 colleges; includes Council-funded and non-Council funded provision

Table 4. Distribution of students in each age group (%) by notional level of qualification

	1994-95						
	% of age group studying at each level						
Level	**under 16**	**16-18**	**19-20**	**21-24**	**25-59**	**60+**	**Total**
1 & entry	14	7	11	16	20	13	15
2	18	28	20	21	18	8	20
3	4	56	39	26	18	7	29
4 & 5	0	2	12	10	7	1	6
not specified	64	7	17	26	37	72	30
Total	**100**	**100**	**100**	**100**	**100**	**100**	**100**

	1995-96						
	% of age group studying at each level						
Level	**under 16**	**16-18**	**19-20**	**21-24**	**25-59**	**60+**	**Total**
1 & entry	20	9	17	23	26	18	21
2	20	28	20	21	18	8	20
3	5	55	34	22	16	6	25
4 & 5	0	1	10	8	6	1	5
not specified	55	7	19	27	35	66	29
Total	**100**	**100**	**100**	**100**	**100**	**100**	**100**

Source: individualised student record (ISR) 1994-95 and 1995-96

Coverage: 1994-95; 373 colleges, 1995-96; 413 colleges; includes Council-funded and non-Council funded provision

Students studying qualifications at different notional levels are allocated to the highest level at which they are studying

Recruitment: prior attainment

Table 5. Percentage of 16 and 17 year old students by level of prior attainment* 1995-96

Age 16	Other FE colleges % of students with				Sixth form colleges % of students with			
Sex	1-19 points	20-29 points	30+ points	foundation target 1	1-19 points	20-29 points	30+ points	foundation target 1
F	11	14	26	48	4	6	16	75
M	17	18	25	39	6	8	18	69
All	**14**	**16**	**26**	**44**	**5**	**7**	**17**	**72**

Age 17	Other FE colleges % of students with				Sixth form colleges % of students with			
Sex	1-19 points	20-29 points	30+ points	foundation target 1	1-19 points	20-29 points	30+ points	foundation target 1
F	10	11	20	59	3	3	10	83
M	14	13	19	53	4	4	12	81
All	**12**	**12**	**19**	**56**	**3**	**4**	**11**	**82**

Source: individualised student record (ISR) 1995-96
Coverage: 178 colleges
Age calculated as at 31 August 1995
*Level of prior attainment calculated from students' qualifications on entry recorded on the ISR as follows:
- foundation target 1 is attainment of 5 GCSEs at grades A-C or equivalent
- for those students not achieving foundation target 1, a points score was calculated from their GCSEs, from 7 points for a grade A down to 1 point for a grade G; point scores were then banded for the purpose of presentation. A student can have achieved 30 or more points but not achieved foundation target 1 if, for example, they have achieved 4 grade Bs and 2 grade D GCSEs

Recruitment: adult students receiving benefit

Table 6. Percentage of adult students with tuition fees waived* by sex

Sex	1994-95 on benefit *	1994-95 ABE or ESOL*	1995-96 on benefit *	1995-96 ABE or ESOL*
	% of students			
F	18	6	19	5
M	18	5	18	4
All	**18**	**6**	**18**	**4**

See notes under table 9

Table 7. Percentage of adult students with tuition fees waived* by age group

Age group	1994-95 on benefit *	1994-95 ABE or ESOL*	1995-96 on benefit *	1995-96 ABE or ESOL*
	% of age group			
19	16	3	17	3
20	20	4	21	3
21-24	21	5	22	4
25-29	22	6	21	5
30-39	20	6	19	5
40-49	16	5	15	4
50-59	18	6	16	4
60+	13	9	16	8

See notes under table 9

Table 8. Percentage of adult students with tuition fees waived* by ethnic group

Ethnicity	1994-95 on benefit *	1994-95 ABE or ESOL*	1995-96 on benefit *	1995-96 ABE or ESOL*
	% of ethnic group			
Bangladeshi	23	23	33	35
Black African	45	12	47	13
Black Caribbean	37	6	44	5
Black other	35	13	45	7
Chinese	15	29	16	26
Indian	22	16	26	12
Pakistani	25	35	29	21
White	18	4	17	3
Other - Asian	24	23	27	19
Other	31	13	31	15

See notes under table 9

Table 9. Percentage of adult students with tuition fees waived* by notional level of qualification

Level	1994-95		1995-96	
	% of students			
	on benefit *	ABE or ESOL*	on benefit *	ABE or ESOL*
1 & entry	16	6	15	4
2	23	1	23	2
3	20	1	21	1
4 & 5	10	0	13	0
not specified	18	11	17	10

Notes to tables 6 to 9

Source: individualised student record (ISR) 1994-95 and 1995-96

Coverage: 1994-95; 369 colleges, 1995-96; 318 colleges. Council-funded provision only

Adult students are those aged 19 and over as at 31 August of the teaching year

*Students receiving benefit can be identified from the ISR if they have their fees remitted by the college.

On the 1994-95 ISR the term 'benefits' covered unemployment benefit, income support, family credit, disability allowance and housing/council tax benefit. In 1995-96 those on benefits included those on unemployment benefit, income support or means tested state benefit. In both years students who are dependent on someone receiving benefit are included. Fees can also be remitted for students studying adult basic education (ABE) qualifications or English for speakers of other languages (ESOL). These students are shown separately

Recruitment: postcodes (level of deprivation)

Table 10. Percentage of FE students by level of deprivation and age group 1994-95

level of deprivation	'DoE score'	% of students aged		% of wards in England
		16-18	19+	
most deprived	> 15	4	5	2
	> 10 to 15	8	10	5
	> 5 to 10	12	13	8
	> 0 to 5	13	14	11
	> -5 to 0	15	14	19
	> -10 to -5	27	25	40
	> -15 to -10	19	18	14
most affluent	< -15	1	1	0
		100	**100**	**100**

Source: individualised student record (ISR) 1994-95; Department of the Environment (DoE) index of local conditions

Coverage: 410 colleges; Council-funded provision only. A high score indicates a deprived area, a negative indicates an affluent area; see *Widening Participation in Further Education: Statistical Evidence* for details of how the deprivation score is calculated

Retention

Table 11. In-year retention rates by mode, sex and by age group 1994-95

	% retained			
	FT		PT	
Age	F	M	F	M
16	89	87	84	86
17	91	89	86	88
18	90	89	86	89
16-18	90	88	85	87
19	90	88	87	89
20-24	88	86	88	87
25+	89	87	91	90
19+	89	87	90	90
Total	**90**	**88**	**90**	**89**

See notes under table 14

Table 12. In-year retention rates by mode, sex and by ethnic group 1994-95

	FT				PT			
	age 16-18		age 19+		age 16-18		age 19+	
	F	M	F	M	F	M	F	M
Ethnicity	%	%	%	%	%	%	%	%
Bangladeshi	89	87	87	83	90	85	91	86
Black African	91	88	87	85	87	87	88	84
Black Carribean	87	82	87	83	83	81	89	86
Black other	84	81	87	83	84	82	88	89
Chinese	92	92	89	90	91	85	88	87
Indian	94	91	89	86	91	88	90	88
Pakistani	92	86	78	79	89	84	88	83
White	90	88	89	87	85	88	90	90
Other - Asian	91	90	88	86	82	86	89	86
Other	**87**	**86**	**88**	**85**	**86**	**83**	**88**	**85**

See notes under table 14

Table 13. In-year retention rates by notional level of qualification and by age 1994-95

Full-time students: % retained

Age group	entry level	level 1	level 2	level 3	level 4	unknown level
		notional level of qualification being studied				
16	86	82	85	91	98	88
17	89	83	84	92	98	91
18	89	82	82	91	91	90
19	90	84	82	90	94	89
20-24	85	82	81	87	95	88
25+	84	86	85	88	94	88
Total	**86**	**84**	**84**	**91**	**94**	**89**

Part-time students: % retained

Age	entry level	level 1	level 2	level 3	level 4	unknown level
		notional level of qualification being studied				
16	85	85	84	85	91	86
17	85	85	86	88	94	87
18	84	85	86	88	92	88
19	85	85	86	88	94	89
20-24	85	85	86	87	93	89
25+	86	88	89	90	94	92
Total	**85**	**87**	**87**	**89**	**93**	**91**

See notes under table 14

Table 14. In-year retention rates for adult students by mode and by payment of tuition fees 1994-95

Payment of tuition fees	% retained FT	% retained PT
Fees waived - student receiving benefit	85	81
Fees waived - unwaged dependant of any people receiving benefits	87	88
Fees waived - student's primary learning goal is adult basic education or English for speakers of other languages	80	87
Fees waived as a result of local college policy	86	92
Fees refunded	79	80
Tax relief for vocational programmes	89	91
Fees waived - other funding	86	94
Fees paid in full	92	91

Source: individualised student record (ISR) 1994-95

Coverage: 373 colleges; includes Council and non-Council funded provision

All students on programmes of more than 12 weeks in duration are included in the analysis

Students count as retained if they have completed or are continuing one or more of the qualifications they studying for

Further details are provided in *Widening Participation in Further Education: Statistical Evidence* to be published in autumn 1997

Achievement rates

Table 15. Achievement rates (%) by mode, sex and by age group 1994-95

	FT				PT			
	F		M		F		M	
Age group	fully achieved	partially achieved	fully achieved	partially achieved	fully achieved	partially achieved	fully achieved	partially achieved
16	49	26	46	25	57	9	57	9
17	60	25	56	25	58	11	57	12
18	61	22	56	22	57	10	58	13
19	62	19	58	19	57	9	59	12
20-24	62	17	58	16	60	8	62	8
25+	61	17	56	16	64	8	66	6
All	**59**	**22**	**54**	**21**	**63**	**8**	**64**	**7**

See notes under table 18

Table 16. Achievement rates (%) by mode and by ethnic group 1994-95

	FT		PT	
Ethnic group	fully achieved	partially achieved	fully achieved	partially achieved
Bangladeshi	52	22	66	8
Black African	45	21	43	10
Black Carribean	44	20	48	9
Black other	46	22	53	9
Chinese	52	23	56	9
Indian	52	24	55	9
Pakistani	54	19	62	7
White	59	22	63	8
Other - Asian	51	22	54	10
Other	49	19	46	8
All	**57**	**22**	**62**	**8**

See notes under table 18

Table 17. Achievement rates (%) by mode and by notional level and type of qualification

notional level	type	FT	PT
level 1 and entry	GNVQ	59	62
	NVQ	62	58
	other	67	59
	total	66	59
level 2	GCSE	71	58
	GNVQ precursor	65	50
	GNVQ	65	55
	NVQ	57	56
	other	64	63
	total	67	59
level 3	GCE A/AS level	72	49
	GNVQ precursor	80	73
	GNVQ	66	67
	NVQ	53	53
	other	70	60
	total	72	57
level 4 and 5	NVQ	74	53
	HNC/HND	62	75
	other	65	62
	total	66	64
level not known		64	68
all levels		**68**	**62**

Partial achievement counts as half a full achievement

Achievement rates for each qualification are calculated separately in this table and not combined into an achievement rate for the student

Table 18. Achievement rates (%) by mode and by payment of tuition fees 1994-95

	FT		PT	
Payment of tuition fees	**fully achieved**	**partially achieved**	**fully achieved**	**partially achieved**
Fees waived - student receiving benefit or is an unwaged dependant of someone receiving benefit	52	19	52	11
Fees waived - student's PLG is adult basic ed or ESOL	74	7	59	9
Fees waived as a result of local college policy	57	18	71	6
Fees waived or refunded for other reasons	52	10	66	7
Fees paid in full	66	14	65	7

Notes to tables 15 to 18

Source: individualised student record (ISR) 1994-95

Coverage: 369 colleges; Council-funded provision only

Achievement rates are calculated as a percentage of final year students who have completed their qualifications

Fully achieved: the student has achieved all of their completed qualifications

Partially achieved: the student has achieved at least half their completed qualifications or has achieved at least half the credits or modules towards their final qualification

Student destinations

Table 19. Destinations of students in further education colleges by mode 1994-95

	FT students			PT students		
Student destination	**students (000s)**	**% (including unknown)**	**% (excluding unknown)**	**students (000s)**	**% (including unknown)**	**% (excluding unknown)**
Further education	62.6	17	37	127	12	48
Higher education	53.9	14	32	9.4	1	4
Employment	40.2	11	24	109.1	10	41
Other	12.2	3	7	17.6	2	7
Unknown	204.7	55		837.3	76	
Total	**373.7**	**100**	**100**	**1,100.50**	**100**	**100**

Source: individualised student record (ISR) 1994-95

Coverage: figures grossed up for all colleges from 383 colleges; Council-funded provision only

Destinations included for all students completing their qualifications in 1994-95